Bugs

by Annabelle Lynch

W
FRANKLIN WATTS
LONDON • SYDNEY

Franklin Watts

First published in Great Britain in 2015 by The Watts Publishing Group

Copyright © 2015 The Watts Publishing Group

Series editor: Julia Bird
Series consultant: Catherine Glavina
Series designer: Peter Scoulding

HB ISBN: 978 1 4451 3865 7
PB ISBN: 978 1 4451 3869 5
Library ebook ISBN: 978 1 4451 3867 1

Dewey number: 570

MIX
Paper from
responsible sources
FSC® C104740
www.fsc.org

Printed in China

Franklin Watts
An imprint of
Hachette Children's Group
Part of The Watts Publishing Group
Carmelite House
50 Victoria Embankment
London EC4Y 0DZ

An Hachette UK Company
www.hachette.co.uk

www.franklinwatts.co.uk

Contents

What are bugs?

Bugs are little animals.

There are billions of
bugs in the world!

A bug's body

Bugs have a hard body. They usually have six legs and wings.

8

Touchy
feely

Many bugs have
two feelers. They
use their feelers to
touch and smell.

Eggs

Bugs hatch from
tiny eggs.

The mother bug lays
lots of eggs at a time.

Eating

Bugs eat all sorts of things. Butterflies suck up the nectar in flowers.

Flying
bugs

Many bugs can fly.
Dragonflies can fly
backwards!

Water
bugs

Some bugs can skate
on top of water
without going under.

Hidden
bugs

Some bugs are the same colour as the place where they live. This helps them hide.

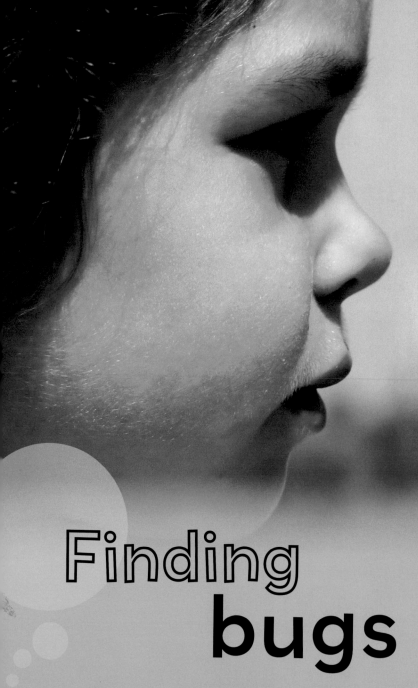

Finding bugs

Bugs are everywhere!
Look for them on
plants or under stones.

Word bank

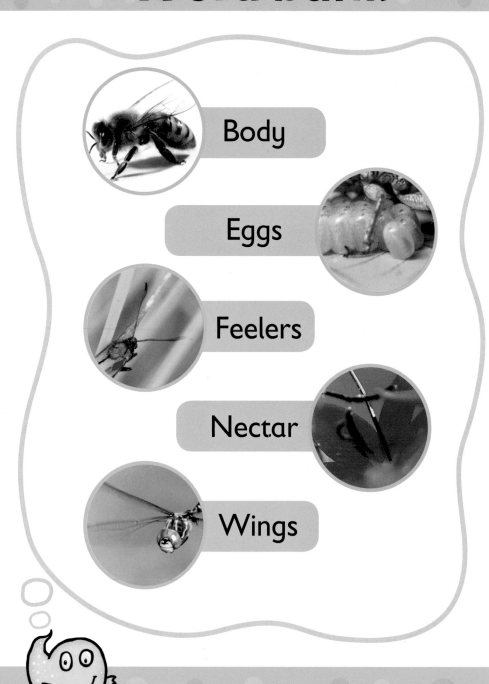

Body

Eggs

Feelers

Nectar

Wings

Quiz

1. Bugs have

a) two legs
b) four legs
c) six legs.

2. Bugs use their feelers to

a) eat and drink
b) touch and smell
c) move around.

3. Butterflies suck up

a) nectar
b) water
c) other bugs.

Turn over for answers!

Notes for adults

TADPOLES are structured to provide support for newly independent readers. The books may also be used by adults for sharing with young children.

Starting to read alone can be daunting. **TADPOLES** help by providing visual support and repeating words and phrases. These books will both develop confidence and encourage reading and rereading for pleasure.

If you are reading this book with a child, here are a few suggestions:

1. Make reading fun! Choose a time to read when you and the child are relaxed and have time to share the book.

2. Talk about the content of the book before you start reading. Look at the front cover and blurb. What expectations are raised about the content? Why might the child enjoy it? What connections can the child make with their own experience of the world?

3. If a word is phonically decodable, encourage the child to use a 'phonics first' approach to tackling new words by sounding the words out.

4. Invite the child to talk about the content after reading, returning to favourite pages and pictures. Extend vocabulary by examining the Word Bank and by discussing new concepts.

5. Give praise! Remember that small mistakes need not always be corrected.

Answers

Here are the answers:

1.c 2.b 3.a

Index